How the Major Stock Indexes Work
From the Dow to the S&P 500

Peter K. Ryan

ROSEN PUBLISHING®
New York

To my parents, Peter and Carol, for giving me a wonderful and blessed life, and to my brother, Chris, and sister, Emily, for your lifelong support

Published in 2013 by The Rosen Publishing Group, Inc.
29 East 21st Street, New York, NY 10010

First Edition

YA
332.6322
RYA

Library of Congress Cataloging-in-Publication Data

Ryan, Peter K.
How the major stock indexes work: from the Dow to the S&P 500/Peter Ryan.—1st ed.
    p. cm.—(Real world economics)
Includes bibliographical references and index.
ISBN 978-1-4488-6789-9 (library binding)
1. Stock price indexes. 2. Stocks—Prices. 3. Stock price forecasting. I. Title.
HG4636.R93 2013
332.63'222—dc23

2011047777

Manufactured in the United States of America

CPSIA Compliance Information: Batch #S12YA: For further information, contact Rosen Publishing, New York, New York, at 1-800-237-9932.

Contents

INTRODUCTION

In August 2008 unsettling news began to develop about Lehman Brothers, then a leading financial services firm. The press began reporting that Lehman Brothers had been exposed to substantial financial risk from investments it had made in the subprime mortgage market between 2004 and 2007. In response to the risks that it faced, Lehman had announced that it was planning to reduce its workforce and sell some parts of its business to make up for the losses it anticipated. This was followed a few days later with news that it had losses in the billions of dollars and that it was looking for a buyer for its core businesses. Finally, on September 9 Lehman announced that there was no suitable buyer for its business, causing Lehman Brothers' stock price to fall more than 45 percent.

This devastating drop in Lehman Brothers' stock price and the continued release of bad news about why Lehman was collapsing caused a major panic in the financial world and a major

Stock boards show details about shares on stock indexes, including price, price change, bid and ask prices, and the total trading volume of the day.

sell-off of the entire stock market. By the end of October 2008, the Dow Jones Industrial Average, one of the leading and best known stock markets, used to judge the health of the stock indexes, had dropped nearly three thousand points, almost 25 percent of its total value.

The unique events of the September and October 2008 market crash show connections between the events that brought down Lehman Brothers and the resulting market panic that followed. The tools that allow us to see the impact of Lehman Brothers on the stock market are called stock indexes.

CHAPTER ONE

UNDERSTANDING STOCKS

Stock indexes are baskets of different stocks of many different companies all bundled together into one representative value, allowing investors to have an indicator of the current health of a sampling of the marketplace. To understand what a stock index is, you first must understand what stocks and the stock markets are. Stocks, also called securities or shares, are pieces of ownership of a company. The purchasers of stocks become shareholders in the company, and their ownership gives them special rights regarding that company, including the right to vote on various decisions and, in some cases, the right to a share of the company profits. When someone purchases stock in a company, he or she becomes a partial owner of that company.

There are many companies that sell their shares to the public and many investors who purchase shares. Typically, companies that do sell shares to the public tend to sell many shares to many investors. Companies sell shares to the public to raise money to finance their operations, grow, and prosper. Just about anyone

The First Stock

The first publicly traded stock was the Dutch East India Company, which began trading in the Netherlands in 1602. The company was chartered by the government of the Netherlands to establish regular trade with Asia. The company was a joint stock company that had private, public, and government investment. Traders formed derivatives based on the stocks that were traded on the Amsterdam Exchange for 196 years, until the date of its final closure. The company paid investors a dividend annually, which is considered a contributing factor to the demise of the company.

can purchase shares of publicly traded companies, provided they have a brokerage account.

People purchase shares in companies because they hope to see the money they invest in a company grow and provide a stable return. They purchase shares in specific companies because they believe those companies have products or services that are valuable and thus likely to yield a better return than other companies. Investors always seek the maximum return with minimal risk of loss of value on an investment.

Stock Markets

Stocks are bought and sold on stock markets, marketplaces where people come together to trade a wide variety of different shares of many different companies. Stock markets provide a range of services that streamline the process of trading shares.

On the floor of the New York Stock Exchange, brokers move about to meet with specialists to trade specific stocks.

Stock markets provide rules that are structured to govern transactions so that all participants understand what is being traded. Stock markets also offer transparency, which is information about the history of all trades in all shares traded on the exchange. Finally, stock markets offer liquidity, which means

they bring lots of parties to the table and thus a lot of potential trading volume, which ultimately makes finding the fair market price more efficient.

The largest and most well-known stock market in the United States, and arguably the world, is the New York Stock Exchange, or NYSE. The NYSE was formed in New York City in 1752 with the signing of the Buttonwood Agreement. A group of stock brokers agreed to create a common exchange where all parties involved could meet to trade stocks. Creating a standard time and location for trading would allow more buyers and sellers to come together to arrange more trades and thus stimulate increased trading activity and investment.

Before the formation of the exchange, buyers and sellers had to meet with a broker to arrange a trade. After the formation of the exchange, buyers and sellers could easily go to the exchange during business hours and find a broker and a counterparty to arrange the trade.

As time passed, stock exchanges evolved and became more sophisticated. The rules and regulations that governed the practices and standards of the exchanges became more complex and efficient at protecting the interests of all the parties involved. In addition, government entities began oversight and regulation of stock exchanges to ensure that the public was well protected.

Bulls and Bears

In the language of stock trading, there are two names that have been given to the two classic types of stock investors: bulls and bears. Investors who are optimistic and believe the market is good and likely to go up are called bulls. Investors who are pessimistic about the market and believe the market is likely to go down are called bears. When people say that they feel "bullish" about a particular stock, they are saying that they believe the stock will go up. The opposite is true for someone who feels "bearish" about a stock.

Bulls buy stocks and hope to make money predicting that the market will go up. Bears try to make money or cut their losses believing that the market will go down. Bulls tend to be aggressive buyers and look for big upward moves in the market to invest. Bears tend to be aggressive sellers and look for big downward moves in the market to invest.

There is another kind of investor called a pig. Pigs are typically very aggressive, impulsive, and greedy, and they don't do all the homework that is required of diligent investing. Pigs look for quick turnarounds and seek to make fast money. There is an adage on Wall Street: "Bulls make money. Bears make money. Pigs get slaughtered." This saying represents the disdain that diligent bulls and bears have for pigs who too often act before thinking and buy or trade stock without doing the proper research.

Companies that list their shares for public sale have legal and regulatory requirements to deliver specific information to the public about their financial status. Each quarter, publicly traded companies are required to report their financial status. The reporting requirement makes it possible for investors to make decisions based on the data presented in the reports and for investors to compare the performance of one company against another.

Comparative Analysis

Comparing one company to another requires a frame of reference, which is usually done on the basis of financial performance. For instance, you can compare beverage makers

Just as consumers may choose products, analysts compare stocks of the companies that make those products based on a variety of criteria, including quantitative and qualitative analysis.

such as the Coca-Cola Company to PepsiCo because they both manufacture similar products. You could make informed comparisons about each company's financial health because the products compete with each other. However, how do you

A trader on the New York Stock Exchange compares the movement and performance of a group of similar stocks in an attempt to predict future prices.

compare companies that are in different industries, such as consumer products producer Apple Inc. to Coca-Cola? You can evaluate their absolute performance, meaning you can look at their bottom-line profitability, and determine whether they're financially sound.

Comparative analysis is at the core of financial decision making. Stock analysts are professionals who study companies' financial performance and then sell their research and recommendations to investors. However, you can ask three different analysts to look at the same company and get three different opinions. This can occur because each analyst draws his or her own conclusions about financial data, even though the numbers each analyst looks at are identical. This makes profitably trading stock all the more difficult for the average investor.

The NASDAQ booth in Times Square is where journalists televise their reports on the technology-focused index, a competitor to the New York Stock Exchange.

Book Value vs. Market Value

Further complicating the picture is the fact that a stock has a nominal value called the book value, which is the total value of all assets and income of a company. If you divide the book value by the total number of shares issued for a company, you calculate the per-share book value. It is a simple calculation and it makes sense because it says that a share of a company is worth a fraction of the company's income and its assets. However in the real world, stocks are bought and sold at a price that a

The NASDAQ "Big Board" highlights the companies trading on the exchange with the biggest moves of the day.

buyer and seller agree upon, which is called the market price of a stock. Book value and market value are often very different, which is because of the varying opinions of the buyers and sellers of a stock on a day-to-day basis.

So how does one try to make a decision about the value of a stock when analysts can't agree? This is where stock indexes come in. A stock index is a bundle of stocks that are chosen to represent a specific view of an industry, a market, a country, or any other representative population.

CHAPTER TWO
THE DOW

The most famous of all U.S. stock indexes is the Dow Jones Industrial Average, commonly referred to as the Dow or the Dow Jones. The Dow Jones index is a collection of thirty of the most valuable and high-profile public companies in the United States. The Dow is reported as a single number, which goes up or down every day. The movement of that number is watched very closely because it represents the overall health of the biggest companies in the country.

Another prominent index is the Standard & Poor's 500, more commonly known as the S&P 500, or just the S&P. The S&P 500 is a collection of five hundred companies that are the biggest and healthiest across a range of industries in the United States. Like the Dow, the S&P 500 is listed as a single numerical value, which people also watch very closely because it represents the daily movement of five hundred of the most valuable companies in the United States. The Dow and the S&P 500 are only two out of many thousands of stock indexes worldwide. Other major indexes around the world include the

Traders use displays such as these to monitor the real-time conditions of major indexes around the world.

Nikkei (Japan), FTSE (Britain), DAX (Germany), Hang Seng (Hong Kong), and the CAC (France).

Stock Prices

Stock prices move constantly. From the opening of the market at 9:30 AM EST to the closing at 4:00 PM, stock prices fluctuate as buyers and sellers transact stocks at prices that they think are fair. Stock prices are determined by the willingness of a buyer and a seller to trade shares for cash at a negotiated price. Because all buyers and sellers are interested in getting the best price possible, it is assumed that all transactions are occurring at the best prevailing market price at the time of the transaction. The price that someone can get for a stock at 10:00 AM may not be the same price he or she can get that same stock for at 2:00 PM. This is because of the dynamic pricing that occurs as buyers and sellers actively negotiate to find satisfactory transaction prices. This is the nature of a marketplace.

Other factors that can influence the price of a stock are news stories about the economy, news about a particular company, politics, the weather, and natural disasters. Stock prices are very sensitive to changing outside factors, as well as to the price movements of other stocks. For example, the stock prices of Coca-Cola and PepsiCo are very strongly related because they sell similar products in the same markets. If the price of Coca-Cola's stock drops, it is likely that the price of PepsiCo will be affected as well. This connection is important because it allows individuals to make estimates about the movement of one stock on the basis of the movement of another.

Stock Correlation

The interrelatedness of stocks, also called correlation, increases in accuracy and certainty as the number of stocks you observe increases. The correlation between ten stocks within the same industry is likely to be much higher than the correlation between ten stocks in different industries. Additionally, the correlation between one hundred stocks in the same industry is likely to be higher than the correlation between ten stocks in

The Hong Kong Stock Exchange, shown here before opening for the trading day, is the third largest in Asia. It has several indexes that track large groups of stocks in the region.

19

the same industry. Differences between companies are reduced as you look at many companies and the underlying common traits that exist between a large group of companies.

The concept of interrelatedness is at the very core of why stock indexes were originally created. Investors needed a way to gauge the overall current health of the stock market by capturing a representative snapshot of the market. This was achieved by the creation of the early stock indexes like the Dow Jones, which served to show a sampling of the most valuable stocks across the stock market. Using the Dow, an investor could make informed decisions about when to buy or sell and what price should be paid based upon the current value of the Dow. It could be assumed that if the Dow were to drop, it was an indicator that the prices of all stocks were likely to go down along with the Dow. The drop in the Dow doesn't cause the drop in other stocks, but the drop of the other stocks is correlated to the drop of the Dow. It is very easy to mistake causality for correlation.

Causality vs. Correlation

Causality means that one event causes another event. Correlation means that one event may happen if another event happens. The drop of the Dow does not cause the drop of other stocks (causality), but other stocks may drop if the Dow drops (correlation). Some stocks can have what is called negative correlation, which means that the rise of one stock may result in the drop of another, and vice versa. Negative correlation, just like normal correlation, doesn't mean that the rise of one stock necessarily will cause the drop of another one. It just means

The Bellwether Index

The S&P 500 is made up of five hundred stocks that represent the overall health of the stock market. It is a bellwether index in that it is a great indicator of the overall health of the stock market.

The stocks are selected from an array of different industry sectors so that the index is representative of the overall stock market. There are very selective criteria that are applied in the evaluation process. They include:

Market capitalization: The company must have an unadjusted market capitalization of at least $4 billion. This means that the total number of shares multiplied by the stock price per share must be equal to or greater than that amount.

Liquidity: The company must have at least 250,000 shares traded every month for the prior 6 months.

Domicile: The company must be based in the United States, have at least half of its business generated in the United States, be listed on the NYSE or NASDAQ, and have a corporate governance structure in the United States.

Public float: At least 50 percent of all the outstanding shares of the company must be owned by the public.

Viability: The company must demonstrate at least four consecutive quarters of positive earnings.

that the observations over time indicate that there is a possibility that the other stock may go down. There is also the possibility that a stock has no correlation to the behavior of another stock, meaning that the movement of one stock is totally arbitrary to the movement of another.

In addition to studying the correlation between individual stocks, people also study the correlation of a stock to a group of stocks or a group of stocks to another group of stocks, and so on. The mathematics required to compute all the correlations is very complex but advances in computing technology have made it very easy to analyze complex sets of correlated data.

Sector Specific Indexes

Not long after the creation of the first stock indexes investors and analysts realized that it would be a good idea to create indexes that track specific sets of stocks. Indexes that tracked utility companies, transportation, manufacturing, retail, and additional industries became very valuable tools for investors because they allowed for a more finely tuned snapshot of a section of the

A mutual fund representative helps customers make investment decisions by providing information about markets, products, and risks that they would not normally be able to access.

marketplace, which theoretically is much more closely in alignment with specific stocks.

Assume that an investor wanted to purchase a particular stock in a transportation company. Before the introduction of the transportation stock index, comprised of many dozens of transportation stocks, the investor had to rely on the current performance of the overall market and the current performance of similar stocks. The addition of the transportation index

Executives at the Vanguard Group, a mutual fund company, create and manage complex investment strategies for their customers, including exchange traded funds and index funds.

provided the investor with a single data point that provided a reference for all stocks in the transportation industry. The investor could now compare an individual stock to the overall performance of many stocks that were very similar. He or she could then make much more informed decisions.

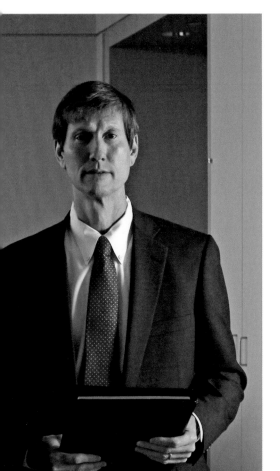

Index Funds

Typically, most indexes are closed to outside investment. They are tools for observation only. However, many companies will create tracking indexes, also called index funds, which are identical in composition and design to the original index. A person can invest in a tracking index that perfectly mirrors the Dow Jones index, for example.

Investors will often choose to buy into index funds instead of individual stocks because they provide risk diversification. Risk, as discussed earlier, is the possibility that the value of your investment may drop below your initial investment amount. Diversification is the practice of spreading your risk across several investments to minimize the specific risk of any one company's stock price movements. If an investor puts $100 into a company and that company drops 10 percent, the loss to the investor would be $10. If an investor put $100 into a stock index made of ten stocks and one of the stocks dropped 10 percent while all of the others stayed the same, the total loss to the investor would be $1. By investing in an index that is made of many different stocks, the investor spreads the risk out. That exposure to the risk posed by a single company is dramatically reduced.

CHAPTER THREE
THE S&P 500

The S&P 500 is a collection of five hundred stocks from companies based in the United States. There is a Standard & Poor's committee that is responsible for the ongoing management and maintenance of the S&P 500, including making sure that it remains a relevant and accurate index. The committee is constantly monitoring the companies in the index, watching the overall market, and watching other companies that are competitors and substitutes for the companies already in the index. It constantly evaluates the mix of companies in the index and at times will add and remove companies that it thinks better represents the broader U.S. market.

When a stock is added to an index, it is given a "weight," which affects its impact on the movement of the overall index. Some stocks are weighted more heavily than others based on parameters that, for the most part, are decided solely by the managers of the index. The determination of the weight is made by the analysis of the index management committee. They are business analysts and mathematicians who determine

Investors attend a conference hosted by Morningstar, an investment rating company that assigns risk ratings to stocks that help investors make better financial decisions.

what stocks should be in the index, what the weight of each stock should be, and how the index should be adjusted when changes to those stocks take place.

Adjusting Stock Indexes

The realignment of index funds, especially large and heavily followed indexes, has an enormous impact on the entire market. It alters the lens through which investors view the marketplace because it forces those investors to question why the experts changed their opinions and thus stimulates new

U.S. Securities and Exchange Commission

The regulatory agency of the federal government that oversees the stock markets is the Securities and Exchange Commission, more commonly known as the SEC. The SEC was created in 1934 to help protect investors from fraud and corruption in the financial markets. The act that created the agency was the Securities Exchange Act of 1934 in reaction to the stock market crash in 1929 and the many investigations that followed, which brought widespread misdeeds to light.

Today, the SEC is charged with regulating the NYSE and NASDAQ, along with many other markets. It works in conjunction with the internal regulatory body FINRA, which is managed by the membership of the major stock markets. The combination of federal oversight with internal controls creates an environment that discourages theft and fraud.

patterns of analysis and decision making. It also forces index fund managers to rebalance their mirrored indexes so that they exactly match the composition of the original S&P. Any time you stimulate a large population of the stock market to behave in any direction, you override the natural flow and process of the market.

When major index funds do announce that they are going to add or remove a stock to or from an index, they have to disclose the information to the public. It is illegal for an index manager to share any secret information before the public is informed. This is designed to prevent "insider trading," which is when someone with privileged or nonpublic information makes an investment before the public is informed for the purpose of making a profit or preventing a loss. The entire industry of people involved in the creation of indexes must follow very strict regulations and rules that protect investors and prevent insiders from making illegal profits.

Quantitative vs. Qualitative Analysis

The methods for evaluating stocks are either quantitative or qualitative. Quantitative analysis is the study of purely financial and technical data about a stock. Qualitative is the study of the company, the industry, and the product that a company sells to evaluate company stock price. Human emotion and intuition are also major factors in analysis. People look at information differently and interpret it based on their own individual perspectives. One investor may look at a stock and see potential for real growth. Another may look at that same stock and see the potential for real loss. Human psychology is at times as significant in the pricing of a stock as are financial metrics.

Sell in May and Go Away

There is an old adage in the investing world, "Sell in May and go away." This phrase got its meaning from the long-run observation that the months of summer and early fall tend to be the lowest performing for the stock market. The adage advises investors to sell their stock in May and go away, most likely for a holiday or vacation.

The market tends to see much slower trading activity in the summer months, largely because so many people take vacation and enjoy the good weather. This is because the major stock markets in the United States are in the Northeast or Midwest, which have very cold and harsh winters. The summer months provide a well-needed dose of sun and fun. So although the adage may seem like superstition, there is merit to its claim.

Individual investor decision making is influenced by day-to-day mood and sentiment. Today, an investor may think that the economy looks good and so will invest money in the market. Tomorrow, that same investor may have a different opinion, which could come from any number of events or thoughts and cause the investor to change his or her mind and sell all investments. Even though there may be available data that may disagree with the emotion of the investor, when an investor gets scared that a stock will fall or becomes overconfident that it will go up, he or she may make decisions based on emotions rather than facts.

Natural disasters like the 2011 Japan earthquake and tsunami often influence the stock market. During the first two days of trading following the tsunami, Japan's Nikkei index fell 16 percent.

Differing Perspectives

This same emotion-based decision making exists in the minds of the millions of investors in the stock market every day. It is reasonable to assume that on any given day there are many millions of different opinions about what will happen in the stock market. However, for every pessimist there is an optimist. For every buyer there is a seller. The natural counter-balancing force of the law of averages makes the day-to-day collective psychology effectively neutral, provided that there is no major outside event that can cause many people to draw the same conclusion simultaneously.

Market Psychology

A great example of the power of collective psychology impacting the marketplace is the effect that a big earthquake can have on the market. When big earthquakes hit a region that is highly populated, there

33

is always the unavoidable loss of life and the interruption of business. When earthquakes damage factories, it usually takes several weeks or months to repair the factories and restore them to regular operations. Because this logic is fairly universal, when word of an earthquake hits the stock market, the immediate reaction is usually a sell-off of any shares of companies based in that area. Investors don't want to be stuck owning shares of a company that is destroyed or impaired, so they try to get rid of those shares as quickly as possible.

This knee-jerk reaction is often overblown but can be enough to severely reduce the share price of a company or even a whole sector of companies. Once accurate and in-depth reports about the actual aftermath of the earthquake start to surface, it is not uncommon for investors to buy back the shares they've sold.

Collective psychology is powerful, and it spreads quickly. It behaves as irrationally as the individual emotional investor, but it is much more powerful than the individual. When an investor begins to understand that a stock price is heavily influenced by the collective psychology, that investor begins to understand the ease with which a healthy stock can fall to extraordinary lows because of false information or investor panic. This realization usually prompts the cautious investor to seek the comfort of diversified investments such as index funds and mutual funds.

CHAPTER FOUR

RISK AND REWARD

Investors who choose to flee the risk of investing in individual stocks for the safety of index funds are trading lower risk for lower potential return. The investor who decides to stick with individual stocks is accepting greater risk in return for the potential for much greater rewards. Stock indexes are created with many different risk reward profiles to meet the needs of different kinds of investors. Some indexes are very safe and stable and provide a very low yield because there is so little at risk. Other indexes are volatile and risky and thus offer the opportunity for a great reward in return for accepting high risk.

The typical investor is usually not a full-time professional investor and will likely have money in the stock market in the form of mutual funds or index funds. Mutual funds and index funds provide risk diversification and the potential for healthy returns based on a moderate risk profile. The typical investor will look at his or her investment portfolio infrequently and will take it on faith from a financial adviser or financial institution that the investment is wise and safe.

Day traders study stock market data and real-time news in order to find insight about trending stocks. Stock indexes are a major part of what traders study to make informed decisions.

People tend to feel that the wisdom of the crowd will prevail and that they are invested in funds that are representative of the overall economy and so likely to be relatively safe and stable. Investors who have invested money in funds are choosing to hand their money to a fund manager who will work very hard to choose the best possible stocks so that the investors' money

will grow. The question remains: how do fund managers choose the stocks that make up their fund?

Shared Data and the Herd Mentality

Fund managers and index managers look at the same raw data, use the same fundamental tools for analysis, and commonly arrive at the same conclusions. They also look to the same industry of third-party investment analysts who specialize in particular companies or industries for additional guidance or insight to help make their decisions. A consequence of fund managers looking at the same data and listening to the same people for guidance is that they can all become panicked or exuberant at the same time.

This is somewhat like a herd of animals fleeing from a perceived threat. A herd of animals grazing in a field can quickly stampede if one of the herd perceives what it believes to be a threat. The animal that detects the threat will send out a signal, and instinctively all the others will try to locate that threat and flee quickly.

Herding animals stay in groups and don't stray too far from each other because there is safety in numbers. This method allows the sheer size of the herd to make up for the relative defenseless nature of an individual animal.

Mutual fund executives, such as David Corkins (*left*) and Scott
Schoelzel, regularly communicate with each other at conferences
to keep informed about markets and trends.

Index Chasing

When a stock index starts falling, the investing community
will start to sell its stock to protect its investment. This selling causes stock indexes to drop further, which can provoke
even more selling by investors. It becomes a growing problem.
Market fear provokes selling, which provokes more fear, which
in turn provokes further selling.

38

Berkshire Hathaway

The billionaire investor Warren Buffett created a company based on his unique and research-oriented approach to investing. The company is called Berkshire Hathaway, and a single share currently costs over $100,000. It takes a moment to absorb that number.

The stock symbol is "brk.a." If you go to a computer and open an Internet browser you can go to Yahoo! Finance or Google Finance to look up the stock. Berkshire Hathaway is priced so high, not only because the company is very successful, but also because its stock has never split in the company's history.

Buffett believes that his company stock should be a place to invest money, not a tool for traders to make money with. So the result is a stock price that only a few select investors can afford, cutting out day traders or those looking to make a quick buck. There is a second Berkshire Hathaway stock, called a "B-Class" share, that is somewhat cheaper. It trades around $70 per share, making it a more accessible stock for the average investor.

This cycle can go on until the price of stocks reaches a point where shrewd investors will step in and buy those falling stocks. Buyers of falling stocks are looking for bargains, opportunities to buy otherwise healthy stocks at discounts to their normal prices. Just like the investors who get spooked and start a sell-off, there are buyers who become exuberant over falling prices and can spark a rally.

The problem with investing based on the movement of stock indexes is that investors' decisions are influenced by the same data that influences the entire investing community. This prevents investors from gaining a competitive edge, unless they decide to pursue a strategy that is not shared by any other investors.

If you view the historical performance of the S&P 500 or the Dow, you find that on average both indexes show positive gains in the long run. The time frame of analysis is very important to the evaluation of the quality of an index or a fund. If a stock has one great year followed by five bad ones, is that a good stock to invest in? If a stock index has ten good years followed by three bad ones, is that a sign of a good index or of the overall economy not performing well?

The purpose of a stock index is to relay a signal from the marketplace to the market participants about a group of stocks.

Stock markets and indexes are connected throughout the world.
Prices in New York impact those in Tokyo and elsewhere.

People are emotional and subjective, and they make imperfect decisions. The ways that investors react to the signals sent by the indexes depend on many factors, including the current economic climate and the overall level of economic ease of the investing population. If investors feel that the economy is doing well and that things are generally good, they will interpret downward signals from the indexes with some amount of resilience. However, if the economy is doing poorly and investors are pessimistic about the general outlook, a downward signal from the indexes will be taken with a sense of caution and panic and will likely result in a sell-off.

MYTHS and FACTS

MYTH The stock market is only for the wealthy, and the only way to make money in it is by being connected.

FACT The stock market is accessible to anyone who can open a trading or brokerage account with either a bank or financial services firm. The requirements for opening an account are usually a minimum deposit. From there, you can begin trading as soon as your account is fully set up.

MYTH The stock indexes are much better judges of the market than I will ever be, so I should always invest my money according to the indexes.

FACT Although stock indexes tend to perform reasonably well over the long run, they are far from the best predictors of achieving large returns on investment. There are many times when following an index is the wrong way to go. The best way to invest your money is to research the market, research the companies you plan to invest in, and keep a close eye on your investments so that you can sell them if they start to lose money.

MYTH What goes up must come down. If a stock is rising today, it can fall tomorrow, so I should wait until the stock drops before I invest.

FACT There are some stocks that you can observe over a long horizon, that have had very few down quarters. Some companies are so well run and have such good products or services that they continuously have a rising share price. There is no perfect time to buy a stock. The time to buy or sell depends upon the individual investor's needs.

CHAPTER FIVE

QUANTITATIVE ANALYSIS

Sophisticated traders use stock indexes as critical input for the models and tools they use as the basis of their investment strategies. These tools are used in a process called quantitative analysis. This analysis studies data on the stock market, individual stocks, and stock indexes to find unique perspectives and unique decisions to gain a competitive advantage.

There are various kinds of technical and quantitative analysis. Some traders use charts, some use simple buy-sell outputs, and some go so far as to create computer programs that buy and sell automatically based purely on the movement of the market.

Traders who use quantitative tools assume that they are going to be able to gain some advantage based on the uniqueness of their quantitative model. However, because most models end up assuming the same data, and use the same indexes as inputs to the model, many quantitative models end up computing nearly identical outputs.

Investment Hedging

Stock hedging is the practice of buying a stock and then purchasing a second investment type that reduces the risk of the overall investment. This is typically achieved by investing in stock options, which are contracts that grant buyers the right to buy or sell a stock at a predetermined price at some point in the future.

A call option is the right to buy the stock. A put option is the right to sell the stock. For instance, assume an investor buys one hundred shares of Apple Inc. To hedge that investment, the investor would need to purchase a put option that has a strike price (also called the exercise price) that is equal to the price paid for the initial one hundred shares of Apple. In this example, if the price of Apple drops below the initial purchase amount, the investor has the right to exercise his or her option and sell shares at the option price, thus hedging the loss to zero.

Options aren't free. They have a cost, which is determined by complex mathematical equations. Typically, an option is priced based on the risk of exposure to rising or falling prices. So a safe stock will have low option prices, and a risky stock will have high option prices.

Stock Charts

One way indexes are used is to overlay data in order to provide comparisons. This is done by selecting a time frame of analysis and then laying out a chart of data points from an index

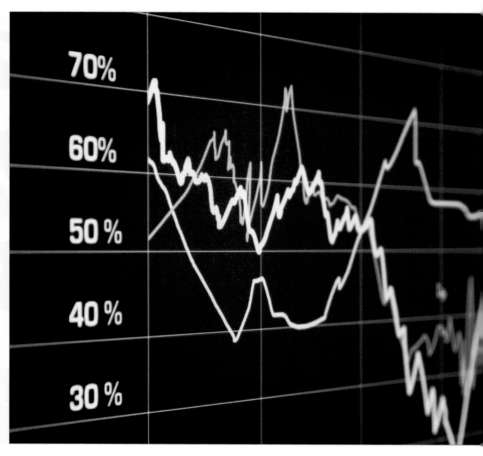

Contrarian investors analyze stock charts just like traditional investors. The difference is that they look for stocks trending against the conventional wisdom.

on the same axes and values of individual stocks. For example, an investor may be interested in purchasing shares in Google but isn't sure if it is the right time to buy. Using a comparative overlay, the investor could compare the chart of Google with the chart of the S&P 500 layered on top. This would show the performance of Google relative to the performance of the S&P 500 for a given time frame.

To get more detailed information about the current price of Google, it would be good for the investor to compare Google to similar companies. The investor could compare Google to individual companies or to an index of high-tech companies. The index would provide a better gauge of the high-tech sector than an individual stock.

After the investor has purchased a stock, it is important to keep track of the performance of the stock. This is done by comparing the stock in question to indexes over time. If a stock starts to underperform on a comparative index, it is usually a very strong signal that it is time to sell that stock.

Looking at the correlation between a stock and the indexes that represent similar companies can reveal interesting behaviors of stock performance. Sometimes, a stock can perform contrary to a particular index because that stock is a substitute for the companies in that index. Some stocks will lag an index, meaning that they will perform similarly to the index but there will be a delay between when the index moves and the stocks follow. Conversely, there are some stocks that can lead an index, meaning that they move ahead of the index.

Contrarian Investing

There are times when investors may disagree with the general consensus of the market. Despite all the index signals and the general trend of the marketplace, investors will sometimes form their own opinion based on the available information.

Warren Buffet's nickname is the "Sage of Omaha" because his overall investment decisions are very wise. His philosophy is to study companies in extraordinary detail and seek true, long-term value.

These investors are called contrarian investors because they bet against the general market.

Contrarian investors apply substantial research and thought to their decisions. They also assume a great amount of risk by betting against the general trend of the market. However, the risk of betting against the market also allows the potential for great profit.

Trading Volume Is an Important Part of Stock Investing

In addition to studying stock price and index price, it is critical to study trading volume. The volume of trading refers to the number of shares that exchange hands over a period of time. Some stocks trade incredibly large numbers of shares per day, and some stocks don't trade very much at all.

Volume is important because it indicates the willingness of individuals to trade a particular stock; it indicates how much a stock might move in order for a stock purchase or sale to be satisfied. It also indicates how likely or unlikely a buyer or seller is to find a counterparty to trade with.

It is also very important to study the average volume of a stock. If a stock trades only ten thousand shares a day and then suddenly starts trading one hundred thousand shares a day for several days in a row, this indicates that something is out of the ordinary. Volume of trading indicates interest in the stock and changing opinions about the stock. Investors should always look for news about a stock when unusual trading volume occurs.

Contrarian investors take the perspective that a stock index can be mispriced by the influence of market psychology. The collective exuberance or panic of the investing community can cause a stock index to become overvalued or underpriced.

Value Investing

Another kind of investor who uses stock indexes extensively is the value investor. Value investors look for stocks that are undervalued by the market and trading at prices below where they should naturally reside based on the financial health of the company. Value investors are not betting against the direction

Value investors use complex charts and mathematical tools to help them determine when a stock is undervalued relative to other stocks in their indexes.

of the market but are looking for opportunities where the market has mispriced a stock.

Value stocks can be index laggards or index leaders. Or they can just be out of alignment for a variety of reasons. Value investors will look at the current price of a stock, at the underlying financials to determine if there is a business-level problem, and then at the index to determine where it should be.

Index Variations

To accommodate the various technical differences between stocks that comprise an index, many index managers will create multiple versions of the same index with different methods for calculating the value. For instance, there are three different versions of the S&P 500: the market-capitalization version, the total return version (which includes the stock dividends of the components), and the net return version (which accounts for dividends and taxes). These versions exist because of varying opinions within the investing community about the impact that dividends and taxes have on stock valuations.

CHAPTER SIX

NEW TECHNOLOGIES

The best way to bring together all the theories and concepts about how the major stock indexes work is to look at historical examples of stock market events. The two events that we are going to use are the 1987 stock market crash and the 2010 "flash crash." These two examples show that the fundamental causes of each crash are very similar, even though the series of events and the technical mechanisms that led to both crashes were very different.

October 19, 1987

In October 1987, stock markets around the world were beginning to show signs of weakness. In 1987, many stock markets had evolved in sophistication and interconnectedness, creating strong links between the movements of all global markets. Events and market activity affecting Asian stock markets were now having a direct impact on actions in Europe and the United States. This had not been the case only twenty years earlier. This

Wall St. panic

Los Angeles Times

Monday, October 19, 198_   Daily 25¢

Bedlam on Wall St.

The New York Times

Late Edition

...ares Sold

...ains of Last
Wiped Out

S PLUNGE 508 POINTS, A DROP OF 22.6%;
LLION VOLUME NEARLY DOUBLES RECORD

EW YORK POST

CT. 20, 1987   Founded by Alexander Hamilton in 1801   25 CENTS

RAS

ll Street's

cks nation

DAILY ● NEW

NEW YORK'S PICTURE NEWSPAPER®

PANIC

Dow drops through floor — 508.32

COMPLETE COVERAGE

October 19, 1987, is now known as Black Monday. The Dow Jones index fell 22 percent, its single worst day in American history.

was made possible by advancements in computer and network technologies that were put to work in the stock markets, and enabled a new wealth of information sharing.

Technology and Market Impact

The advances in information technology made it possible to trade shares much more rapidly and with much more information about the real-time status of other markets around the world. Before the availability of electronic market data, traders had to use telephones, couriers, and crude communication tools to gather information about the status of other markets. The speed of information retrieval was slow, and the scope of data available was limited. A savvy trader would be able to sift through mountains of "telex" communication data, but it took time, effort, and labor to do so.

Before the introduction of newer information technologies, there was correlation between the movements of stock markets, but the correlation was weak. Movements in one market could be totally isolated from movements in another market. This was due to the fact that there was very little information available about what was happening in those foreign markets. Therefore, very few people looked to compare the impact of foreign stock movements with U.S. stock movements.

In the 1960s and 1970s, the New York Stock Exchange was a paper-based market. All transactions took place via handwritten papers, which were physically exchanged between brokers. The pace of trading was increasing and the ability of the traders to keep up with the speed of trading using pens and paper was reaching its limit. The use of pneumatic tubes that would shuttle papers in carrier plugs was a common trading tool on

Exchange Traded Funds

An exchange traded fund (ETF) is a form of mutual fund or index fund that is traded on a stock market. Unlike traditional mutual or index funds, which require investors to purchase shares directly from the fund itself, an ETF is freely tradable on a variety of stock markets.

ETFs are currently very popular investment vehicles because they are very easy to buy and sell, the ease of selling being the primary draw. Traditional mutual and index funds have windows of opportunity for investors to buy in and sell out of positions in the fund. Additionally, traditional funds operate on a previous-day price basis, meaning that if you buy into a mutual fund today, you will get the price of the fund that is determined at the end of the previous trading day, at 4:00 NK EST. Despite the movement of the stock market before that time, the price you get is unknown until the market closes. Investors would much rather be able to sell their fund shares whenever they want, and ETFs allow for that.

ETFs come in all forms, from basic mutual funds and index funds to exotic triple-leveraged short funds. The more exotic funds are not appropriate for inexperienced investors because they are very volatile and can be very hard to understand.

the NYSE. Electronic tickers had been in use for decades, delivering a steady stream of information about stocks, but information moved very slowly and was often many hours behind the actual state of the market.

Today, technology enables stock indexes around the world to connect at the speed of light, creating a truly global and interdependent market.

Globally Connected Markets

By 1987, world markets had begun sharing massive quantities of data with each other across new high-speed intercontinental cables. This flood of new data allowed traders to read much more deeply into the activity of other markets. Information about stock indexes in other countries was now readily available and made the process of estimating the movement of world markets based on the events in other countries common practice. Traders were able to see the prices and movements of stocks around the world in real time.

Another major addition to stock trading in the 1980s was the introduction of "program trading." Program trading is computerized trading based on external inputs from the movements of the stock market. Brokerages and trading firms would employ computer programmers and mathematicians to create complex mathematical formulas that would use stock market signals such as the S&P 500 to initiate stock trading routines. For example, a program might be designed to watch the S&P 500. If the S&P 500 dropped ten points, the program might be tasked to sell $1 million worth of a particular stock.

Program trading enabled traders to create sophisticated models that took into account many different analysis points. It used many different inputs such as the Dow and the S&P 500 (among a list of many others) to create programs that were initiated and left to run on their own.

In early October 1987, the general mood of investors about the global economy was nervous, nearing on panicky. In the first two weeks of October, stock markets around the world began experiencing sustained days of selling activity, driving markets lower. The intensity of the selling was never before seen in terms of the percentage drop of the markets. On October 19, 1987, a day now referred to as "Black Monday," the Dow Jones Industrial Average fell 508 points, about 22 percent of its total value. Not only was this the biggest point drop ever, but it was also the biggest percentage decline in a single day.

Program Trading

What made the speed and intensity of the decline possible was the speed of information delivery from the markets real-time

In today's electronic world, traders must monitor enormous amounts of data in order to keep pace with the speed of the marketplace. Information is delivered in real time, which, in an instant, influences indexes around the world.

data, the speed of the delivery of index data, and the corresponding speed of trade execution by program trading systems. It was a compounding dilemma. Stocks dropped, which pushed the indexes lower, which caused programs to sell stocks, which pushed the indexes lower, and so on. Program trading systems had been designed to operate within the context of normal day-to-day market conditions. An event like Black Monday hadn't been assumed possible. Safeguards against such a scenario had not been included in the programs because the likelihood of them being needed was assumed to be nearly zero.

In addition to the programs reacting to the negative signals from the major stock indexes, professional money managers, fund managers, and mutual funds all sold out of fear of a total market collapse. The indexes seemed to be in a total free fall across every industrial sector. There was no escaping the power of the total market sell-off that day. By the end of October 1987, global stock markets had all dropped anywhere from 40 to 60 percent from where they were just a month before.

The Flash Crash

The "flash crash" of 2010 was similar to Black Monday 1987 in that information technology played a major role. Unlike Black Monday, which was an entire day of trading that resulted in the

The "flash crash" of May 6, 2010, sent stocks plummeting and raised questions about the dangers of computer-based trading.

sell-off of 508 points, the flash crash took place within less than an hour and resulted in a sell-off of 1,000 points and the almost immediate recovery of 600 points.

The flash crash occurred on May 6, 2010, at 2:45 PM EST. The causes are still being debated within some academic circles, and the

Short Selling

One of the most difficult concepts for new investors to grasp is short selling. Selling a stock short means that a seller sells shares to a buyer, but the seller doesn't own the shares that he or she is selling. The reason for this is that the seller is betting that the price of the stock will drop.

After the trade occurs, there is a three-day window of settlement during which both parties transfer cash and shares to complete the deal. When a short sale occurs, the seller doesn't have the shares initially. He or she has to find someone to buy them from. The lender of the stock charges the borrower a fee, and the seller delivers the shares to the buyer.

There have been occasions when short sellers have "oversold" a stock, meaning that they have sold more shares to buyers than the total number of shares that exist. This happens when short sellers use call options to offset their short. They claim that although they don't have the shares now, they own the right to buy shares in the future at a guaranteed price, which is an artificial way of "holding" the shares.

Short selling requires careful study of complex stock charts. These investments can be devastating if the trade goes in the wrong direction.

final consensus from the investigation by the U.S. Securities and Exchange Commission is still being criticized. The chain of events that caused the crash happened so quickly that it is hard to pinpoint the causes of the crash. One of the challenges of studying this incident is the complexity of all the elements leading to such a dramatic sell-off.

Index Futures

There are many kinds of financial instruments that are traded in addition to stocks. One that played a role in the events of the flash crash was index futures. A future allows a person to pay someone today at today's price for the right to buy an asset at some point in the future, regardless of what the future price might be.

An index future is a contract between a buyer and seller in which the seller agrees to sell the underlying index to the buyer at a predetermined date in the future for a predetermined price. The buyer has to pay the seller an amount now to secure the deal. When done, the seller is obligated to deliver on the date at the agreed-upon price.

Computer experts monitor stock trading systems to ensure that transactions are running properly. In the technologically advancing marketplace, information technology experts are almost as critical to the health of stock indexes as the traders themselves.

Index futures in the S&P 500 are traded on the Chicago Board Options Exchange (CBOE). The index futures are traded just like ordinary stocks. There are buyers and sellers, and they use the marketplace to trade and settle all their transactions.

Origin of the Flash Crash

The flash crash was started by a single trade originating in the S&P 500 futures index in which a very large number of contracts were sold in a short amount of time. This activity caused a chain reaction of program trades that spanned across different asset types and markets. High-frequency traders (HFTs), who specialize in rapid computer-generated trades, were the first to see their selling programs triggered. These triggers caused the HFT trading programs to kick into their natural selling routine, which caused the major indexes to drop. This in turn caused other program trades to initiate, which further eroded the market.

In many ways, Black Monday and the flash crash had many similarities. The automation of trades certainly played a major role in both events. The biggest difference between these events is the speed with which they occurred and the degree of the interconnectedness between stock indexes around the globe. The natural progression of the markets has resulted in increased automation and advancement in complexity of relationships of various kinds of financial instruments.

The increase of interconnectedness of the stock markets and derivative markets provides very powerful capabilities for market participants. In the case of the flash crash, the interconnectedness of the marketplaces coupled with the lack of fail-safe mechanisms in trading programs brought about the rapid stock crash and equally rapid stock recovery. This is a unique event that has brought about substantial reform within the stock market. The flash crash was the kind of event that market regulators use to craft new regulations to protect investors.

Stock indexes still play a vital role in helping investors determine when to buy and sell stocks. The complexity of the marketplaces has increased along with the sophistication of the traders involved. The fact remains that despite our best efforts, there is no way to predict the future. We can only study the past. It is because of this that stock indexes will always play a vital role in stock markets.

Ten Great Questions
to Ask an Economist

1. Which indexes should I follow to get a better sense of how the U.S. and global economies are doing?

2. Why is the Dow Jones the most commonly used index when it only has thirty stocks in it?

3. What is a stock dividend, and why should I care about it?

4. What is the difference between a stock and a stock option?

5. How do I find out if a stock is in an index?

6. Why is the stock market so difficult to predict?

7. How do I choose a stock brokerage firm?

8. What kind of stock should I buy if I want my money to grow over the long term?

9. Is it better to buy a stock that is in the S&P 500 or in the Dow?

10. What indexes should I look at if I want to track the performance of foreign markets?

GLOSSARY

Big Board Another name for the New York Stock Exchange. It earned this name because it has historically been the premier marketplace for listing the biggest and most valuable stocks in the United States.

book value The current value of a company based on the value of its assets and income.

call option A stock option that gives the owner the right to purchase a particular stock at a point in the future at a predetermined price.

derivative A financial instrument that is based on the value of an underlying asset. A stock option is a derivative of a stock.

dividend A payment that is made to a stockholder each quarter, paid to investors out of the quarterly profits that a company earns.

float The total amount of all outstanding shares of a company that are in the hands of the public.

index weight A value assigned to each stock in an index to maintain the overall stability of the index when stocks are added or deleted from the index.

liquidity The availability of ample stock interest both to buy and sell within a particular marketplace.

market capitalization The value of a company calculated as the total number of shares outstanding multiplied by the current stock price.

put option A stock option that gives the owner of the option the right to sell a particular stock at a point in the future at a predetermined price.

return on investment The amount of money that an investment earns relative to the initial investment amount.

risk The exposure that an investor has to the potential for loss of initial investment. Highly risky investments generally offer higher returns because the potential for loss is great.

shares outstanding The total number of shares that a company has authorized and issued. Shares outstanding are made of shares owned by the company and the float.

stockbroker A professional financial services provider who specializes in facilitating the buying and selling of stock. Stockbrokers are the conduit between an investor and the stock market, enabling the investor to access the market.

stock A piece of ownership of a company. Companies raise money by creating shares and selling those shares to investors. The company retains a large portion of the shares to maintain control of the company. The shares that are sold to the public are called the float.

volatility Volatility is the measurement of stock price movement over time. High volatility means that a stock's price tends to swing widely; low volatility means that a stock's price tends to stay within a narrow price range.

FOR MORE INFORMATION

Canadian Stock Exchange
The Exchange Tower
130 King Street West
Toronto, ON M5X 1J2
Canada
(888) 873-8392
Web site: http://www.tmx.com/en
The Canadian Stock Exchange is the premier stock market in
Canada. Its Web site provides detailed information about the
exchange and the stocks on the exchange.

Certified Financial Planner Board of Standards
1425 K Street NW
Suite 500
Washington, DC 20005
(800) 487-1497
Web site: http://www.cfp.net
A certified financial planner (CFP) is someone who has
undergone substantial training and testing to qualify as an
expert in financial planning. The Certified Financial
Planner Board of Standards is responsible for managing the
membership requirements and maintaining the CFP status.

Chartered Financial Analyst Institute
560 Ray C. Hunt Drive
P.O. Box 2083
Charlottesville, VA 22903-0668
(800) 247-8132
Web site: https://www.cfainstitute.org
A chartered financial analyst (CFA) is an expert in his or her field and has gone through extensive training and testing to achieve the CFA designation. There is substantial learning material on the Chartered Financial Analyst Institute Web site.

FINRA Investor Education Foundation
1735 K Street NW
Washington, DC 20006-1506
(202) 728-8348
Web site: http://www.finrafoundation.org
The FINRA Investor Education Foundation provides underserved Americans with financial information and educational material to help improve their financial management skills. In collaboration with the Consumer Federation of America and Channel One, it launched Generation Money in January 2009 to help teach secondary school students about the power of compounding and other important financial lessons.

NASDAQ
The NASDAQ Stock Market
One Liberty Plaza
165 Broadway
New York, NY 10006
(212) 401-8700

Web site: http://www.nasdaq.com/investing
The NASDAQ is the second leading stock market in the United States. Its Web site has a very well-rounded and informative Investing Insight section that provides educational resources.

New York Stock Exchange (NYSE) Learning Center
20 Broad Street, 17th floor
New York, NY 10005
Web site: http://nyse.nyx.com/en/learningcenter
The NYSE is the premier stock exchange in the world. The NYSE Learning Center is a source of information about stocks, the stock market, and financial management.

Web Sites

Due to the changing nature of Internet links, Rosen Publishing has developed an online list of Web sites related to the subject of this book. This site is updated regularly. Please use this link to access the list:

http://www.rosenlinks.com/rwe/sidx

FOR FURTHER READING

Bateman, Katherine R. *The Young Investor: Projects and Activities for Making Your Money Grow*. Chicago, IL: Chicago Review Press, 2010.

Baumohl, Bernard. *The Secrets of Economic Indicators: Hidden Clues to Future Economic Trends and Investment Opportunities*. 2nd ed. Upper Saddle River, NJ: Pearson Education, 2008.

Beach, Byron. *Stock Matters for Kids: An Introduction to Stock and Ownership*. San Francisco, CA: OneShare, 2006.

Bochner, Arthur. *The New Totally Awesome Money Book for Kids*. New York, NY: Newmarket Press, 2007.

Connolly, Sean. *The Stock Market*. Mankato, MN: Amicus Publishing, 2010.

Foster, Jill Russo. *Cash, Credit, and Your Finances: The Teen Years*. Seattle, WA: Amazon Digital Services, 2009.

Furgang, Kathy. *How the Stock Market Works* (Real World Economics). New York, NY: Rosen Publishing, 2010.

Hansen, Mark Victor. *The Richest Kids in America: How They Earn It, How They Spend It, How You Can Too*. Miami, FL: Hansen House Publishing, 2009.

Karlitz, Gail. *Growing Money: A Complete Investing Guide for Kids*. New York, NY: Price Stern Sloan, 2010.

Kramer, Jim. *Jim Cramer's Stay Mad for Life: Get Rich, Stay Rich* (Make Your Kids Even Richer). New York, NY: Simon & Schuster, 2007.

Lowell, James. *Investing from Scratch: A Handbook for the Young Investor*. New York, NY: Penguin, 2007.

Orr, Tamra. *A Kid's Guide to the Economy*. Hockessin, DE: Mitchell Lane Publishers, 2009.

Orr, Tamra. *A Kid's Guide to Stock Market Investing*. Hockessin, DE: Mitchell Lane Publishers, 2009.

Roth, Alan S. *How a Second Grader Beats Wall Street: Golden Rules Any Investor Can Learn*. Hoboken, NJ: Wiley, 2011.

Sember, Brette McWhorter. *The Everything Kids' Money Book: Earn It, Save It, and Watch It Grow!* Avon, MA: Adams Media, 2008.

Thompson, Helen. *Understanding the Stock Market*. Broomall, PA: Mason Crest Publishers, 2010.

BIBLIOGRAPHY

Bamford, Janet. *Street Wise: A Guide for Teen Investors.* Princeton, NJ: Bloomberg Press, 2000.

Bernstein, William J. *The Investors Manifesto.* Hoboken, NJ: John Wiley & Sons, 2010.

Biggs, Barton. *Wealth, War & Wisdom.* Hoboken, NJ: John Wiley & Sons, 2008.

Dalton, John M. *How the Stock Market Works.* 3rd ed. New York, NY: New York Institute of Finance, 2001.

Dodd, David L., and Benjamin Graham. *Security Analysis.* New York, NY: McGraw-Hill, 2009.

Ferri, Richard A. *All About Index Funds: The Easy Way to Get Started.* New York, NY: McGraw-Hill, 2002.

Hebner, Mark T. *Index Funds: The 12-Step Program for Active Investors.* Irvine, CA: IFA Publishing, 2005.

Levinson, Mark. *Guide to Financial Markets.* Princeton, NJ: Bloomberg Press, 2003.

Malkiel, Burton G. *The Random Walk Guide to Investing: Ten Rules for Financial Success.* New York, NY: W. W. Norton & Company, 2003.

Tigue, Joseph R. *The Standard & Poor's Guide to Long-Term Investing.* New York, NY: McGraw-Hill, 2003.

INDEX

About the Author

Peter Ryan earned his M.B.A. at the Lally School of Management and Technology at Rensselaer Polytechnic Institute and his B.A. at Villanova University. He worked on the New York Stock Exchange and American Stock Exchange in the specialist business between 1999 and 2004 and currently runs an IT consulting business.

Photo Credits

Cover (banner) © istockphoto.com/Lilli Day; cover and interior graphics (graph) © istockphoto.com/Andrey Prokhorov; cover, p. 1 (quotes) © istockphoto.com/Ash Waechter; p. 5 Stephen VanHorn/Shutterstock.com; pp. 6, 16, 27, 35, 44, 52 (NYSE silhouette), 62–63 Mario Tama/Getty Images; pp. 8–9 Spencer Platt/Getty Images; p. 11 Daniel Acker/Bloomberg/Getty Images; pp. 12–13 Daniel Acker/Bloomberg/Getty Images; pp. 14, 60–61 Jin Lee/Bloomberg/Getty Images; p. 15 Joe Corrigan/Getty Images; p. 17 Hou Jun/Xinhua/Landov; pp. 18–19 Laurent Fievet/AFP/Getty Images; pp. 22–23 Bradley C. Bower/Bloomberg/Getty Images; pp. 24–25 Tim Shaffer/Reuters/Landov; pp. 28, 53 © AP Images; pp. 32–33 Kimimasa Mayama/Bloomberg/Getty Images; pp. 36–37 Jason Alden/Bloomberg/Getty Images; p. 38 Matthew Staver/Bloomberg/Getty Images; pp. 40–41 Kim Kyung–Hoon/Reuters/Landov; pp. 46–47 © istockphoto.com/Anthia Cumming; p. 48 Scott Olson/Getty Images; p. 50 Ermek/Shutterstock.com; pp. 56–57 Georges DeKeerle/Hulton Archive/Getty Images; pp. 58–59 Philippe Wojazer/Reuters/Landov; pp. 64–65 Tim Boyle/Bloomberg/Getty Images; interior graphics (people) © istockphoto.com/studiovision; interior graphics (side arrows) © istockphoto.com/Darja Tokranova; interior graphics (cogs) © istockphoto.com/Chan Fu Soh; interior graphics (circled arrows) © istockphoto.com/articular; back cover and interior graphics (up arrows) © istockphoto.com/Dean Turner.

Designer: Michael Moy; Editor: Nicholas Croce;
Photo Researcher: Amy Feinberg